Low Carb High Protein Cookbook

Easy And Delicious High Protein Low Carb Diet Recipes For Burning Fat

Copyright ©

Disclaimer

All the material contained in this book is provided for educational and informational purposes only. No responsibility can be taken for any results or outcomes resulting from the use of this material.

While every attempt has been made to provide information that is both accurate and effective, the author does not assume any responsibility for the accuracy or use/misuse of this information.

You should always consult a doctor regarding any medical conditions, the information in this book is not intended to diagnose or treat any medical condition or illness.

Table of Contents

Introduction

The low carb diet is one of the most proven and effective diets for losing weight. The low carbohydrate diet is simple to follow, and is based on consuming foods that are mainly low in carbohydrates. Consuming less carbs in your diet, has been shown to increase the fat burned by your body, and is overall a very effective weight loss diet.

Low carb dieting tips for beginners:

- Include vegetables and lean meats (fish and chicken) in your diet. Most vegetables and meats contain low amounts of carbs, and can control your appetite.

- Avoid starchy foods like pasta, potatoes, and rice. These foods have high amounts of carbs!

- Stick to drinking water, most other drinks like juice may include sugars that you may not be aware of.

- Most processed foods have added sugars, it is recommended to avoid preserved and processed foods for this reason.

All of the recipes in this cookbook are low in carbs, high protein, and taste great. Because of how easy these recipes are to make, these low carb high protein recipes are perfect for beginners, or busy people.

We hope you enjoy these low carb high protein recipes, good luck!

Chapter 1: High Protein Low Carb Chicken Recipes

Lime Garlic Chicken

Ingredients

4 boneless, skinless chicken breast halves

2 tablespoons butter

1 tablespoon olive oil

2 teaspoons garlic powder

3 tablespoons lime juice

3/4 teaspoon salt

1/4 teaspoon black pepper

1/4 teaspoon cayenne pepper

1/8 teaspoon paprika

1/4 teaspoon garlic powder

1/8 teaspoon onion powder

1/4 teaspoon dried thyme

1/4 teaspoon dried parsley

Directions

In a small bowl, mix together salt, black pepper, cayenne, paprika, 1/4 teaspoon garlic powder, onion powder, thyme and parsley. Sprinkle spice mixture generously on both sides of chicken breasts.

Heat butter and olive oil in a large heavy skillet over medium heat. Saute chicken until golden brown, about 6 minutes on each side. Sprinkle with 2 teaspoons garlic powder and lime juice.

Cook 5 minutes more, stirring frequently to coat evenly with sauce.

Nutrition: 220 Calories; 10g Fat; 28g Protein; 2g Net Carbs per 1/4 of recipe

Creamy Chicken Bake

Ingredients

8 boneless chicken breasts, flattened

Salt, pepper and garlic powder

1/4 cup olive oil

1 pound pork sausage

1 stalk celery, chopped

8 ounces cream cheese, softened

8 ounces cheddar cheese, shredded, divided

1 pound fresh mushrooms, sliced

1/4 cup fresh parsley, chopped

Directions

Season the chicken; brown in hot oil. Set aside. Brown the sausage and celery; drain and cool slightly. Heat the oven to 350F°.

Spray a 9x13 inch baking pan and put the mushrooms in the bottom. In a bowl, mix the sausage, cream cheese, 4 ounces cheddar cheese and the parsley.

Spoon this mixture over the mushrooms and smooth with a spoon; place the chicken on top.

Cover and bake 30 minutes. Remove the cover; top with the rest of cheese. Bake 15 minutes until the cheese is melted and browned and the chicken is fully cooked.

To serve, put the chicken on a plate cheese side up; spoon the mushroom mixture over the top.

Nutrition: 599 Calories; 43g Fat; 49g Protein; 3g Net Carbs per 1/8 of recipe

Creamy Chicken Chowder

Ingredients

3 large chicken breasts

1 package of bacon

2 cups of chicken Broth (low carb/sodium)

1 8oz package of cream cheese

2 cups of heavy cream

2 tbsp butter

1/2 large onion

1/2 bell pepper

1 stalk of celery chopped.

8 oz steams and pieces mushrooms

2 tsp minced garlic

1 tsp salt

1 tsp black pepper

1 tsp basil

1 tsp thyme

2 tsp garlic powder

Directions

Turn slow cooker on low and add vegetables and 1 1/2 cups of chicken broth in the slow cooker with butter and a pinch of Salt, cover.

Cut bacon into small pieces and cook until very crisp. Remove from pan and put aside. Leave 2 tbsp of Bacon grease in the bacon and place chicken breasts in the pan to sear on both sides.

Remove Chicken and cut into small cubes. Use remaining 1/2 cup of chicken broth to de-glaze the pan, pour this into the slow cooker.

Add bacon, chicken, heavy cream, cream cheese and seasonings, stirring until well blended.

Cook on low setting for 6 hours, stirring well before serving.

Nutrition: 382 Calories; 31g Fat; 20g Protein; 5g Net Carbs per 1/12 of recipe

Honey Mustard Chicken Breasts

Ingredients

4 boneless chicken breasts

2 tbsp Extra virgin olive oil

2 tbsp mustard

2 tbsp tarragon - dry

2 tbsp honey

Directions

Mix wet ingredients with chicken in dish or plastic bag.

Marinate chicken for up to 24 hours before cooking. Preheat oven to 350 for 20 minutes. Place chicken in glass dish or pan, using remaining marinade to put beneath chicken.

Bake chicken for approximately 30 minutes or until chicken is no longer pink.

Nutrition: 138 Calories; 5g Fat; 20g Protein; 2g Net Carbs per 1/4 of recipe

Dill Chicken Breasts

Ingredients

4 boneless, skinless chicken breast halve

1 teaspoon garlic powder

3 tablespoons butter

1/2 cup whipping cream

2 tablespoons capers, drained and rinsed

1 teaspoon lemon pepper

1 teaspoon salt

1 teaspoon dried dill weed

Directions

Season chicken breasts with lemon pepper, salt, dill weed, and garlic powder.

Melt butter in a large skillet over medium heat. Place breasts in skillet, and increase heat to medium-high.

Turn chicken frequently, until brown, about 5 minutes. Reduce heat to medium, and cook 5 to 7 minutes, until breasts are cooked through. Remove chicken to a warm serving platter, and cover with foil.

Return skillet to stove, and increase heat to high. Whisk in whipping cream, whisking continuously until reduced to sauce consistency, about 3 minutes.

Remove from heat. Stir in capers. Pour sauce over chicken, and serve.

Nutrition: 313 Calories; 21g Fat; 28g Protein; 2g Net Carbs per 1/4 of recipe

Balsamic Basil Chicken Breasts

Ingredients

6 skinless, boneless chicken breast halves

1 teaspoon garlic salt

ground black pepper to taste

2 tablespoons olive oil

1 onion, thinly sliced

1 (14.5 ounce) can diced tomatoes

1/2 cup balsamic vinegar

1 teaspoon dried basil

1 teaspoon dried oregano

1 teaspoon dried rosemary

1/2 teaspoon dried thyme

Directions

Season both sides of chicken breasts with garlic salt and pepper.

Heat olive oil in a skillet over medium heat; cook seasoned chicken breasts until chicken is browned, 3 to 4 minutes per side. Add onion; cook and stir until onion is browned, 3 to 4 minutes.

Pour diced tomatoes and balsamic vinegar over chicken; season with basil, oregano, rosemary and thyme.

Simmer until chicken is no longer pink and the juices run clear, about 15 minutes and a instant-read thermometer inserted into the center reads at least 165 F

Nutrition: 196 Calories; 7g Fat; 24g Protein; 7g Net Carbs per 1/6 of recipe

Mediterranean Chicken Breasts

Ingredients

6 skinless, boneless chicken breast halves

6 ounces tomato basil feta cheese, crumbled

1/4 cup Italian-style dry bread crumbs, divided

Directions

Preheat oven to 350 F. Lightly grease a 9x13 inch baking dish.

Place chicken breasts between 2 pieces of waxed paper. Gently pound chicken with flat side of meat mallet until approximately 1/4 inch thick; remove wax paper. Place 1 ounce of feta cheese in the center of each chicken breast, and fold in half.

Spread 2 tablespoons bread crumbs in the bottom of the prepared baking dish. Arrange chicken in the dish, and top with remaining bread crumbs.

Bake 30 minutes in the preheated oven, or until chicken is no longer pink and juices run clear.

Nutrition: 224 Calories; 8g Fat; 32g Protein; 4.5g Net Carbs per 1/6 of recipe

Marinara Chicken

Ingredients

2 pounds boneless, skinless chicken breasts

4 cloves garlic, peeled and crushed

4 tomatoes, chopped or one 14.5-ounce can low-sodium tomatoes, drained

4 medium ribs celery, diced

2 small zucchini, diced

1 bell pepper, cored, seeded, and diced

One 18-oz jar low-sodium marinara sauce

1 tsp dried basil

1 tsp dried thyme

Directions

Place the chicken in the slow cooker; add the garlic, tomatoes, celery, zucchini, and pepper.

Pour the marinara sauce over all, and sprinkle the basil and thyme on top.

Set the slow cooker on low and cook for 6 to 7 hours. Before serving, shred the chicken with a fork.

Nutrition: 178 Calories; 4g Fat; 27g Protein; 8g Net Carbs per 1/8 of recipe

Chicken Creole

Ingredients

8-12 chicken thighs, skin removed

1 cup celery, chopped, 4 ounces

1 red pepper, sliced, 4 ounces

1 green pepper, sliced, 4 ounces

Small onion, chopped, 2 1/2 ounces

4 ounce can mushrooms, drained

14.5 ounce can diced tomatoes

1 teaspoon garlic powder

1 teaspoon granular Splenda or equivalent liquid Splenda

1 teaspoon Cajun Seasoning

1/2 teaspoon paprika

1 teaspoon salt

1/2 teaspoon pepper

Hot sauce, to taste

Directions

Put the chicken in a crockpot. Mix the remaining ingredients and pour over the chicken. Cook on low 7-8 hours.

Nutrition: 325 Calories; 22g Fat; 26g Protein; 4g Net Carbs per 1/8 of recipe

Spicy Grilled Chicken Breasts

Ingredients

3 chicken breasts

1 tsp salt

2 garlic cloves

1 tbsp ginger

1/2 onion chopped

1 jalapeno pepper, minced

3/4 cup unsweetened coconut milk

1 cup frozen peas

Directions

Heat a non-stick frying pan, cut chicken in thirds and then add chicken to skillet. Let chicken cook without moving it for 3 minutes, to let the chicken brown.

Flip over and add the garlic, ginger, onion and jalapeno. Stir and cook until onion is started to get soft.

Add the coconut milk and stir. Cook on lower heat for another 7-10 minutes.

Toss in the peas and cook for another two minutes until the chicken is fully cooked and no longer pink.

Nutrition: 320 Calories; 11g Fat; 44g Protein; 9g Net Carbs per 1/4 of recipe

Chicken And Swiss Cheese Casserole

Ingredients

1 pound boneless chicken breasts or tenders, cut into bite-size pieces

12 ounces ham, cut into cubes

6 ounces Swiss cheese, shredded

Salt and pepper, to taste

8 ounces cream cheese, softened

1/2 cup heavy cream

1 clove garlic, minced

1/8 teaspoon freshly ground pepper

1/8 teaspoon dill

2 teaspoons chives

1 tablespoon fresh parsley, chopped

Directions

Put the chicken, ham and cheese in a greased 12x7 inch baking dish. Season with a little salt and pepper.

In a medium bowl, blend the heavy cream into the cream cheese until smooth. Stir in the garlic, pepper, dill, chives and parsley. Pour over the meat and cheese and stir everything together.

Bake at 350F° for about 40 minutes until bubbly and the chicken is fully cooked.

Let stand about 10 minutes before serving to allow some of the liquid to soak back into the sauce.

Nutrition: 754 Calories; 55g Fat; 60g Protein; 4g Net Carbs per 1/4 of recipe

BBQ Chicken Wings

Ingredients

3 pounds chicken wings (15 wings)

Salt and freshly ground black pepper

½ cup hickory flavored barbecue sauce

1-1/2 tablespoons dijon mustard

1 tablespoon red wine vinegar

1 tablespoon honey

1 tablespoon hot sauce

Directions

Preheat oven to 400 degrees. Cut off and discard wing tips. Cut each wing at joint to make two sections.

Place wing pieces on foil lined baking sheet. Season to taste with salt and pepper. Bake for about 20 minutes or until chicken is a light, golden brown.

Transfer chicken wings to slow cooker. In a bowl, whisk together the barbecue sauce, mustard, vinegar, honey and hot sauce.

Pour over the chicken wing pieces and toss gently until completely coated.

Cover and cook on LOW for 4 to 4-1/2 hours or until the wings are tender.

Stir at least once to make sure that the wings are evenly coated with the sauce.

Nutrition: 331 Calories; 22g Fat; 7g Carbohydrates; 24g Protein; per 1/8 of recipe

Chapter 2: High Protein Low Carb Beef Recipes

Black Pepper And Garlic Flank Steak

Ingredients

1 (2 pound) flank steak or round steak

3 cloves garlic, minced

1/2 cup soy sauce

2 tablespoons vegetable oil

2 tablespoons ketchup

1 teaspoon dried oregano

1 teaspoon ground black pepper

3 cloves garlic, minced

1/2 cup soy sauce

2 tablespoons vegetable oil

2 tablespoons ketchup

1 teaspoon dried oregano

1 teaspoon ground black pepper

Directions

In a small bowl, mix together garlic, soy sauce, oil, ketchup, oregano, and black pepper. Pierce meat with a fork on both sides.

Place meat and marinade in a large resealable plastic bag. Refrigerate 8 hours, or overnight.

Preheat grill for medium-high heat.

Lightly oil the grill grate. Place steak on the grill, and discard marinade.

Cook for 5 to 8 minutes per side, depending on thickness. Do not overcook, as it is better on the rare side.

Nutrition: 222 Calories; 9g Fat; 4g Carbohydrates; 30g Protein; per 1/6 of recipe

Adobo Chipotle Steak

Ingredients

4 (8 ounce) beef sirloin steaks

1 lime, juiced

1 tablespoon minced garlic

1 teaspoon dried oregano

1 teaspoon ground cumin

2 tablespoons finely chopped canned chipotle peppers in adobo sauce

adobo sauce from canned chipotle peppers to taste

salt and pepper to taste

Directions

In a small bowl, mix the lime juice, garlic, oregano, and cumin. Stir in chipotle peppers, and season to taste with adobo sauce.

Pierce the meat on both sides with a sharp knife, sprinkle with salt and pepper, and place in a glass dish. Pour lime and chipotle sauce over meat, and turn to coat. Cover, and marinate in the refrigerator for 1 to 2 hours.

Preheat grill for high heat.

Lightly brush grill grate with oil. Place steaks on the grill, and discard marinade.

Grill steaks for 6 minutes per side, or to desired doneness.

Nutrition: 342 Calories; 18g Fat; 4g Carbohydrates; 38g Protein; per 1/4 of recipe

Beef Stir Fry

Ingredients

8 oz top sirloin beef

3 cloves garlic

2 tsp soy sauce

1/2 of a leek

Dash of salt and pepper

Directions

Slice beef and combine with garlic, soy sauce, and pepper and marinate at room temperature for 20 minutes.

Slice leeks and set aside.

In a skillet, heat oil over high heat and begin to brown the beef. Add leeks and salt and stir until leeks are wilted and meat cooked.

Nutrition: 151 Calories; 5g Fat; 3g Carbohydrates; 21g Protein; per 1/4 of recipe

Spicy Jalapeno Sirloin

Ingredients

1 1/2 pounds top sirloin steak

4 jalapeno peppers, stemmed

4 cloves garlic, peeled

1 1/2 teaspoons cracked black pepper

1 tablespoon coarse salt

1/4 cup lime juice

1 tablespoon dried oregano

Directions

Combine jalapenos, garlic, pepper, salt, lime juice and oregano in a blender. Blend until smooth.

Place steak in a shallow pan or large resealable plastic bag. Pour jalapeno marinade over the steak, and turn to coat. Cover pan or seal bag; marinate in the refrigerator 8 hours or overnight.

Preheat an outdoor grill for high heat, and lightly oil the grill grate.

Drain and discard marinade. Grill steak 5 minutes per side, or to desired doneness.

Nutrition: 186 Calories; 10g Fat; 3g Carbohydrates; 19g Protein; per 1/4 of recipe

BBQ Short Ribs

Ingredients

4 pounds boneless beef short ribs

13 ounces low carb barbecue sauce

Directions

Place the ribs in a crock pot and pour in the barbecue sauce. Cook on LOW about 8 hours until the meat is tender.

Nutrition: 779 Calories; 58g Fat; 55g Protein; 6g Net Carbs per 1/6 of recipe

Marinated Ginger Steak

Ingredients

4 (8 ounce) beef sirloin steaks, at least 3/4 inch thick

2 tablespoons soy sauce

1 teaspoon ground ginger

1/2 teaspoon salt

1 teaspoon ground black pepper

1 teaspoon dried basil

1 tablespoon prepared yellow mustard

1 teaspoon lemon juice

Directions

Preheat the ovens broiler.

In a small bowl, mix together the soy sauce, ginger, salt, pepper, basil, mustard and lemon juice until smooth. Place the steaks on a broiling pan, and pour 1/4 of the mixture over each one. Rub into the meat.

Broil the steaks for 5 minutes, then turn over and cook to your desired level of doneness.

Nutrition: 296 Calories; 13g Fat; 2g Carbohydrates; 40g Protein; per 1/4 of recipe

Garlic And Herb Beef Tenderloin

Ingredients

5 pound whole beef tenderloin

6 tablespoons olive oil

8 large garlic cloves, minced

2 tablespoons minced fresh rosemary

1 tablespoon dried thyme leaves

2 tablespoons coarsely ground black pepper

1 tablespoon salt

Directions

Prepare beef: Trim off excess fat with a sharp knife. Fold thin tip end under to approximate the thickness of the rest of the roast. Tie with butcher's twine, then keep tying the roast with twine every 11/2 to 2 inches.

Cut silverskin with scissors to keep roast from bowing during cooking. Then, mix oil, garlic, rosemary, thyme, pepper and salt; rub over roast to coat. Set meat aside.

Either build a charcoal fire in half the grill or turn all gas burners on high for 10 minutes. Lubricate grate with an oil-soaked rag using tongs.

Place beef on hot rack and close lid; grill until well-seared, about 5 minutes. Turn meat and close lid; grill until well-seared on second side, another 5 minutes.

Move meat to the charcoal grills cool side, or turn off burner directly underneath the meat and turn remaining one or two burners to medium.

Cook until a meat thermometer inserted in the thickest section registers 130 degrees for rosy pink, 45 to 60 minutes, depending on tenderloin size and grill.

Let meat rest 15 minutes before carving.

Nutrition: 346 Calories; 27g Fat; 2g Carbohydrates; 26g Protein; per 1/13 of recipe

Blue Cheese Peppercorn Steak

Ingredients

1 beef fillet (12 ounces), cut into 3-ounce steaks

3 tbsp crumbled blue cheese

1/4 cup chopped parsley

2 tsp of black, red, and pink peppercorns

Directions

Preheat the oven to 375° F.

In a small bowl, combine the blue cheese and parsley and use a wooden spoon to loosely work into a paste. Cover and refrigerate.

Spread the cracked peppercorns onto a plate. Pat the meat dry and roll in the peppercorns to coat on all sides.

Place a cast-iron skillet or heavy-bottomed ovenproof sauté pan over moderately high heat.

Once hot, place steaks into the dry pan and sear the top and bottom of each steak, 1 to 2 minutes per side.

Place 1 tablespoon of the blue cheese mixture on top of each steak and transfer the pan to the oven. Roast 6 to 7 minutes for rare, 7 to 8 minutes for medium.

Nutrition: 245 Calories; 18g Fat; 1g Carbohydrates; 19g Protein; per 1/4 of recipe

Spiced Roasted Beef Tenderloin

Ingredients

2 (2 pound) beef tenderloin roasts, trimmed

2 tablespoons fresh rosemary

2 tablespoons fresh thyme leaves

2 bay leaves

4 cloves garlic

1 large shallot, peeled and quartered

1 tablespoon grated orange zest

1 tablespoon coarse salt

1 teaspoon freshly ground black pepper

1/2 teaspoon ground nutmeg

1/4 teaspoon ground cloves

2 tablespoons olive oil

Directions

In a food processor, combine rosemary, thyme, bay leaves, garlic, shallot, orange zest, salt, pepper, nutmeg, and cloves. Run machine while adding oil; process until smooth.

Spread mixture evenly over all sides of tenderloins. Place beef in a large glass baking dish. Cover with foil, and refrigerate for at least 6 hours.

Preheat oven to 400F.

Place tenderloins on a rack in a large roasting pan. Roast beef in preheated oven until meat thermometer registers 140 degrees when inserted into center of beef, about 35 minutes.

Remove from oven, and cover loosely with foil; let stand for 10 minutes. Slice beef, and serve.

Nutrition: 683 Calories; 55g Fat; 2g Carbohydrates; 41g Protein; per 1/8 of recipe

Spicy Shredded Beef With Salsa

Ingredients

3 lb beef chuck roast, trim fat

1 tbsp cumin seed

1 tbsp coriander seed

1 tbsp chili powder

1 tsp salt

1 tbsp cayenne pepper

1 cup salsa

2 tbsp water

1 tbsp cornstarch

Directions

Cut roast in half. Combine cumin, coriander, chili powder, salt and red pepper in small bowl.

Rub over roast. Place 1/4 cup salsa in slow cooker; top with one piece roast. Layer 1/4 cup salsa, remaining beef and 1/2 cup salsa in slow cooker. Cover; cook on LOW 8 to 10 hours.

Remove roast from cooking liquid; cool slightly. Trim and discard excess fat from beef. Shred meat with forks.

Let cooking liquid stand 5 minute. Skim off fat. Blend water and cornstarch until smooth.

Whisk into liquid in slow cooker. Cook, uncovered, 15 minutes on HIGH until thickened. Return beef to slow cooker.

Cover; cook 15 minutes or until hot. Adjust seasonings.

Nutrition: 324 Calories; 15g Fat; 44g Protein; 2g Net Carbs per 1/16 of recipe

Beef Tenderloin With Herbs

Ingredients

1 (3 pound) beef tenderloin

2 teaspoons olive oil

2 cloves garlic, minced

2 teaspoons dried basil

1 1/2 teaspoons dried rosemary, crushed

1 teaspoon sea salt

fresh ground black pepper to taste

Directions

Preheat oven to 425 F.

Tie the tenderloin at 2-inch intervals with kitchen string.

Combine oil and garlic in a bowl; brush over meat. Mix basil, rosemary, sea salt, and black pepper together in a bowl; sprinkle evenly over the meat.

Roast beef tenderloin in preheated oven until beginning to firm and is hot and slightly pink in the center, 40 to 50 minutes.

An instant-read thermometer inserted into the center should read 140 degrees F.

Nutrition: 205 Calories; 14g Fat; 1g Carbohydrates; 17g Protein; per 1/12 of recipe

Chapter 3: High Protein Low Carb Pork Recipes

Balsamic Pork Tenderloin With Glaze

Ingredients

1 1/2 lb pork tenderloin

1/4 tsp salt

1/8 tsp black pepper

1/4 cup balsamic vinegar

3 tbsp Splenda brown sugar blend

Directions

Preheat oven to 425F.

Rinse pork and pat dry season with salt and pepper, then brown pork in a skillet until all sides are caramelized. Turn heat to medium low and remove pork from pan.

Add the balsamic vinegar to skillet, stir and loosen up all the brown crusty material from bottom of pan, add the Splenda. Continue to stir until it is fully mixed and forms a glaze, then place pork back in pan turning to coat.

Place pan in roasting pan and place in oven roast for 25 minutes or until pork is cooked. Glaze pork periodically with the remaining glaze in the pan.

Nutrition: 257 Calories; 9g Fat; 7g Carbohydrates; 33g Protein; per 1/6 of recipe

Southwest Pork Tenderloin

Ingredients

2 whole pork tenderloins

4 teaspoons chili powder

1 1/2 teaspoons dried oregano

3/4 teaspoon ground cumin

1/8 teaspoon dried garlic powder

Directions

Mix together chili powder, oregano, cumin, and garlic powder. Rub over the surface of pork. Cover and refrigerate 2-24 hours.

Grill over medium hot coals or broil in oven turning occasionally. Cook for 20-25 minutes until meat is fully cooked. Meat thermometer should read 155-160° F when placed in center.

Nutrition: 170 Calories; 5g Fat; 1g Carbohydrates; 28g Protein; per 1/6 of recipe

Marinated Ginger Pork Chops

Ingredients

6 pork loin chops, 1/2 inch thick

1/2 cup orange juice

2 tablespoons soy sauce

2 tablespoons minced fresh ginger root

2 tablespoons grated orange zest

1 teaspoon minced garlic

1 teaspoon garlic chile paste

1/2 teaspoon salt

Directions

In a shallow container, mix together orange juice, soy sauce, ginger, orange zest, garlic, chile paste, and salt. Add pork chops, and turn to coat evenly. Cover, and refrigerate for at least 2 hours, or overnight. Turn the pork chops in the marinade occasionally.

Preheat grill for high heat, and lightly oil grate.

Grill pork chops for 5 to 6 minutes per side, or to desired doneness.

Nutrition: 136 Calories; 3g Fat; 4g Carbohydrates; 21g Protein; per 1/6 of recipe

Green Chili Pork

Ingredients

2 tbsp ground cumin

1 tsp cayenne pepper

1 tbsp salt

1 tbsp chile powder

1 boneless pork roast (3 lbs)

3 (4 oz each) cans diced green chiles

Juice of 2 limes

9 cloves garlic, crushed

1 cup low-fat, low-sodium chicken broth

1 medium onion, diced

1 tbsp minced fresh cilantro

Directions

Combine spices and rub over pork.

Place pork into slow cooker. Combine remaining ingredients and pour over meat.

Cook on low for 7-10 hours. Remove meat from slow cooker and lightly shred with a fork.

Place back into slow cooker and stir. Drain juice from meat and serve.

Nutrition: 278 Calories; 16g Fat; 28g Protein; 5g Net Carbs per 1/10 of recipe

Pork Loin Roast With Herbs

Ingredients

1 (4-pound) boneless pork loin, with fat left on

1 tablespoon salt

2 tablespoons olive oil

4 cloves garlic, minced

1 teaspoon dried thyme or 2 teaspoons minced fresh thyme leaves

1 teaspoon dried basil or 2 teaspoons fresh basil leaves

1 teaspoon dried rosemary or 2 teaspoons minced fresh rosemary

Directions

Preheat oven to 475 degrees F.

Place the pork loin on a rack in a roasting pan. Combine the remaining ingredients in a small bowl. With your fingers, massage the mixture onto the pork loin, covering all of the meat and fat.

Roast the pork for 30 minutes, then reduce the heat to 425 degrees F and roast for an additional hour.

Test for doneness using an instant-read thermometer. When the internal temperature reaches 155 degrees F, remove the roast from the oven.

Allow it to sit for about 20 minutes before carving.

Nutrition: 209 Calories; 10g Fat; 1g Carbohydrates; 27g Protein; per 1/6 of recipe

Garlic Pork Chops

Ingredients

4 thick cut boneless pork chops

1/4 cup olive oil

1 cup chicken broth

2 cloves garlic, minced

1 tablespoon paprika

1 tablespoon garlic powder

1 tablespoon poultry seasoning

1 teaspoon dried oregano

1 teaspoon dried basil

salt and pepper to taste

Directions

In a large bowl, whisk together the olive oil, chicken broth, garlic, paprika, garlic powder, poultry seasoning, oregano, and basil. Pour into the slow cooker.

Cut small slits in each pork chop with the tip of a knife, and season lightly with salt and pepper.

Place pork chops into the slow cooker, cover, and cook on High for 4 hours. Baste periodically with the sauce.

Nutrition: 275 Calories; 20g Fat; 20g Protein; 4g Net Carbs per 1/4 of recipe

Herb And Lemon Pork Chops

Ingredients

6 (4 ounce) boneless pork loin chops

1/4 cup lemon juice

2 tablespoons vegetable oil

4 cloves garlic, minced

1 teaspoon salt

1/4 teaspoon dried oregano

1/4 teaspoon pepper

Directions

In a large resealable bag, combine lemon juice, oil, garlic, salt, oregano, and pepper. Place chops in bag, seal, and refrigerate 2 hours or overnight. Turn bag frequently to distribute marinade.

Preheat an outdoor grill for high heat. Remove chops from bag, and transfer remaining marinade to a saucepan. Bring marinade to a boil, remove from heat, and set aside.

Lightly oil the grill grate. Grill pork chops for 5 to 7 minutes per side, basting frequently with boiled marinade, until done.

Nutrition: 202 Calories; 10g Fat; 25g Protein; 2g Net Carbs per 1/6 of recipe

Spicy Pulled Pork

Ingredients

2.5 lb pork roast

1 can tomatoes with diced green chiles

1 small can diced green chiles

2 tsp taco seasoning

1 tsp cayenne pepper or to taste

3 cloves of garlic; minced

1/2 cup chopped onion

Directions

Place 1 can of tomatoes with diced green chiles on the bottom of slow cooker. Place pork roast on top.

Mix can of green chiles with the other ingredients and pour on top of the roast.

Set slow cooker on low for 8 hours. Once finished cooking, shred pork and place it back in the slow cooker to mix with the juices.

Nutrition: 250 Calories; 18g Fat; 18g Protein; 2g Net Carbs per 1/12 of recipe

Made in the USA
Middletown, DE
10 November 2019